Whisper in the Woods celebrates the beauty and value of nature by sharing a carefully selected showcase of art, photography and literature. Each issue offers new ways for all of us to *Discover, Explore* and *Appreciate* the natural world we cherish.

Editor/Publisher
Kimberli A. Bindschatel

Founding Designer
Suzanne Conant

Illustrator
Rod Lawrence

Inspiration
Mother Nature

Associate Editor
Denise Baker

Contributors
Eric Alan
Nancy Bordine
Danica Davidson
Erin Fanning
Jan Ferris
Shawn Grose
Darrell Gulin
Dewitt Jones
Janea Little
Rick Pas
Torrey Wenger
Michelle Worden

Webmaster
Stacy Niedzwiecki

Journal Dogs
Kloe & Tucker

Special Thanks
Ken Bindschatel
Patrick Cannon
Dewitt Jones

Cover Photograph
© Darrell Gulin

Printed in the U.S.A.
Progress Printers
Traverse City, MI

Nature Journal

Volume Six, No. Two

To Subscribe:
For current rates, please visit
www.WhisperintheWoods.com
or write to:
Whisper in the Woods Subscriptions
P.O. Box 1014
Traverse City, MI 49685
(866) 943-0153

Change of Address:
The post office will not automatically
forward *Whisper in the Woods* when you
move. To ensure continuous service,
please notify us at least six weeks
before moving. Send your new address
and subscription number to: *Whisper
in the Woods* Subscriptions, P.O. Box
1014, Traverse City, MI 49685.

Submitting art, photography or writing:
Please download our guidelines at
www.WhisperintheWoods.com

We are proud to be affiliated with:

Kalamazoo Nature Center
Kalamazoo, Michigan
www.naturecenter.org

Chippewa Nature Center
Midland, Michigan
www.chippewanaturecenter.org

Ad Sales:
Toll-Free (866) 943-0153
ads@whisperinthewoods.com

Whisper in the Woods®
(ISSN 1543-8821) is published quarterly
by Turning Leaf Productions, LLC. We
strive for accuracy in the articles and hon-
esty in advertising. We reserve the right to
refuse any advertising that is inappropri-
ate or not in harmony with the editorial
policy. Please obtain written permis-
sion before reproducing any part of this
publication. ©2007 All rights reserved.
Registered trademark.

Member, International Regional
Magazine Association

About this issue: (ISBN 978-0-9785820-4-3) Issued Summer 2007

Butterflies and moths may not be scientifically classed together, but as
beauty goes, we admire their "Art on the Wing."

~Kimberli Bindschatel, Editor in Chief

Art on the Wing

Discover

Photographer
Darrell Gulin
7

Explore

Writer
Jan Ferris
18

Appreciate

Artist
Rick Pas
21

Next Issue: Five-Year Commemorative

enjoy Nature.org

Destinations
nature travel destinations to explore in the Great Lakes region, whether you're hiking, paddling or cycling

Calender of Events
plan your outings, from moonlit hikes to cross-country skiing to artist appearances

Seasonal Watch
when and where to find Nature in her finest splendor, from spring wildflower blooms to peak autumn color, let fellow nature lovers know on our blog

Activities
Kids Treehouse, crafts and fun activities, Geocaching destinations

Marketplace
product reviews, from snowshoes to kayaks to backpacks as well as items to purchase

Galleries
post your own photographs, essays and poetry, or browse our featured artist galleries

E-Newsletter
sign up, it's free

Free E-Postcards
send beautiful images to your friends

... *your path to nature!*

www.enjoyNature.org

Brought to you by *Whisper in the Woods* in partnership with the Great Lakes Nature Alliance

Art on the Wing

my thoughts...

Kimberli A. Bindschatel

Kimberli A. Bindschatel
Editor in Chief

Mother Nature's art, so beautifully and perfectly designed, is captivating to any discerning observer. In no other place is it so conspicuous than the wings of a butterfly or moth. Bold colors, intricate designs and shining iridescence grace the world by way of these fascinating insects.

As a child, I would spend hours chasing butterflies with a net. I don't know why. I didn't want to keep one; I had seen collections where butterflies were stuck with pins and held in glass boxes–I had no desire for that. I simply wanted to see them flit on the wind or light on a flower and show me both sides of their magical wings.

To a seven-year-old, the butterfly is like a goddess. She is born a clumsy, ugly creature who magically wraps herself in cotton and emerges a graceful beauty. Doesn't every young girl dream of that fairytale–her own metamorphosis into an adult?

Folklore, fairytale and legend provide many versions of the story, all derived from the amazing miracle that is metamorphosis.

The wonders of Nature never cease. We can obtain lessons from every aspect of Nature if only we take the time to seek them. Some are so apparent while others stay veiled in metaphor to be extracted only by great sages. On either path, Mother Nature, with her infinite wisdom, is our everlasting teacher.

Photo by Kristen Westlake
www.KristenWestlake.com

Jewels on Wings

Black swallowtail butterfly on goldenrod and backdrop of pink cosmos

Darrell Gulin

Mounrning cloak butterfly on rubekia and backdrop of dahlia flowers

Wing details of the scales and design of the underwing
of the giant swallowtail

Spicebush butterfly on freesia flowers

Cecropia moth resting on paper birch tree trunk

American painted lady on a zinnia flower

Close-up wing pattern details of luna moth

Pair of luna moths on lichen-covered tree trunk

Promethea moth female

Black swallowtail butterfly on daisy flowers

Close-up of male luna moth and his antenna

American painted lady butterfly

Buckeye butterfly on russell lupine

Monarch with wings closed resting on zinnia flower bloom

Black version of the eastern tiger swallowtail butterfly on zinnia flower

Photographer's Statement

"Butterflies are self-propelled flowers." –R.H. Heinlein

I have been fascinated with butterflies since I was a child–with their flight, color, and design going from flower to flower. Now these wonderful subjects, along with silk moths, have become my long-time passion to photograph.

Also, butterflies are a good indicator of the quality of our–and their–environment; they need the right temperature, humidity and sunlight. And many species are dependent on specific plant life. Designing a butterfly garden is a way to enjoy these jewels on wings and to help the environment. –*Darrell Gulin*

www.gulinphoto.com

The Magic of Life
Butterflies Teach Us the Dance of Metamorphosis

by Jan Ferris

When I slide my kayak into a lake, I almost always turn left and slowly float clockwise along the shoreline. I scrutinize every plant, every flower, every wave-worn log. It may take me twice as long to get around a lake as the average kayaker. But then, they might miss the young bass following close alongside, the glistening dew snuggled into bright green moss, and the delicate dragonmouth and ladyslipper orchids hiding beneath leatherleaf and cottongrass. Dragonflies whirr past me, dipping and diving as they devour tiny insects.

Butterflies beckon me to follow them, always just out of my camera's reach. They are searching the shoreline, too, for a sweet treat hidden in the flowers: nectar. Antennae sniff it like tiny radar and lead them to a tall bank of joe-pye weed. Settling on the rosy blossoms, they enjoy a snack while warming their wings in the sun. I pause for a moment to examine the perfectly symmetrical design of each wing until the butterfly decides to move to another plant.

One can become entranced watching butterflies float gracefully on the slightest breeze. They symbolize freedom, going where they will in their own sweet time. Maybe that is why we are so attracted to them, envious of them, and why "butterflying" is fast becoming a popular nature hobby, just as birding has. We are attracted to their simple beauty and myriad colors, not even considering what complex and amazing creatures they really are.

Although it is hard for the naked eye to see them, butterfly wings are covered with millions of tiny scales. Moths and butterflies are the only insects with scales, belonging to the order *Lepidoptera*, which means scale-winged. Looking at the beautiful colors and designs of their wings, it is hard to believe that they are actually transparent and that these scales give them their color. "Ground" scales are small and make up the background coloration of the design in butterfly wings. "Cover" scales are larger and more colorful, comprising the main patterns of the design. Each scale is attached by a narrow stalk, and when handled, the scales rub off and appear as a fine powder on your fingers. These loose scales have a slippery, or buttery, texture and help butterflies and moths escape from enemies who grab them by the wings.

Each microscopic scale is a single color, produced either by pigments derived from plants or the way in which they refract and reflect sunlight, which makes them appear iridescent. There are even more colors on their wings that can only be seen by other butterflies.

Another interesting thing about butterfly wings is that their top and undersides can look completely different. While resting with their wings folded up, the coloration of their undersides often camouflages them in their surroundings. They play hide and seek with me, and I pass them by unnoticed until they flutter out of hiding, only to disappear again. The undersides of some butterflies even blend in with the sky so they can't be detected from below.

But the tops of their wings are completely opposite, being bright and flamboyant, as if to say, "Come and get me!" The addition of an eye spot or warning color, however, may send quite a different message to a predator, by mimicking an animal or saying, "Poisonous! Stay away!" For example, monarch caterpillars store distasteful sugar derivatives from poisonous milkweed plants, which carry over to adult butterflies. Experience has taught birds that these orange and black butterflies are nasty tasting, so they usually avoid them. The viceroy butterfly seeks protection by disguising itself as a monarch, with only a couple of subtle differences that birds can't detect. This disguise does occasionally fail them, I noticed, when I found the four wings plucked from a viceroy and scattered beneath a perched praying mantis.

Butterflies in cooler regions may have more black or dark colors on their wings to help them absorb heat more quickly, allowing them to warm up and fly on cool days. Male and female butterflies may have different color schemes, with the males typically being brightly colored and the females being more subdued. Color helps males find a suitable mate.

As I pull my kayak onto shore, I see a group of yellow and black tiger swallowtails gathered in the mud near the landing. They are extracting minerals and moisture from the mud, called "puddling," with their long proboscis, or sucking tube. Getting their wings wet can disable butterflies, so they must use this method to get a drink. They also use their proboscis to suck nectar from flowers, juices from fruit, or moisture from animal droppings. When it is not in use, they curl it up under their body. I am allowed to approach this social gathering a little closer, noticing how they slowly move their wings in contentment as they drink, like a content baby suckling from its mother.

Another symbolic aspect of butterflies is one of transformation and shapeshifting. This is derived from their complex life cycle, changing from a tiny egg, to a caterpillar, to a chrysalis, and finally into a delicate butterfly. This change is called metamorphosis. Even within the caterpillar stage, as they grow they shed their skin several times before making a chrysalis. In Sleeping Bear Dunes, I watched several sizes of monarch caterpillars feeding on their exclusive host plant, milkweed. These caterpillars, or larvae, are smooth with black, yellow and white

achieve a foundation from the idea that we shape, form and develop. In the chrysalis stage of our lives, we need to back off and go deeply within so that creation will be able to come forth strong and in new light. We need to be passive and let things take a natural course in this stage, just as the caterpillar is doing. The new and final form is the winged butterfly, the final expression of life.

Some people call butterflies dancing flowers. Andrews says in his

They symbolize freedom, going where they will in their own sweet time.

stripes. I also found the caterpillars on South Manitou Island, and their shiny green chrysalises stuck to the siding of an old farmhouse. Some students found a monarch chrysalis at the nature center where I worked, so we brought it inside and were privileged to watch the adult butterfly emerge. We then released it to nature to continue the life cycle.

In his book *Animal Speak*, author Ted Andrews compares the process of metamorphosis to the stages in our own lives. Change is inevitable in life, and we should not resist it. Change ensures growth, and we must shed the old before we can come into the new. This is the magic of life that butterflies can teach us. During the egg stage, there is the fertilization process. We give birth–to an idea, an activity, a new quality, anything. Then in the larval stage, we work to

book that butterflies appear to dance as they light upon flowers, awakening a sense of lightness and joy in us. He calls it the dance of joy, but butterflies are actually tasting with their feet as they move around the flowers. They remind us that life is a dance, that we should not take it so seriously, and that we should get up and move–for if we can move, we can dance.

Butterflies have called me to follow them around the lake edges and dance with them down a spring path. They have led me to beautiful flowers and made me pause in sunny meadows. They have taught me patience and humility, and that not all changes in life are traumatic. I have been invited to be a child once again, encouraged to grow into an adult, and I have taken pleasure in admiring art on the wing.

Nature's Surfaces and Textures

Cecropia/Moss

Rick Pas

Luna/Oak

Dogwood/Oak

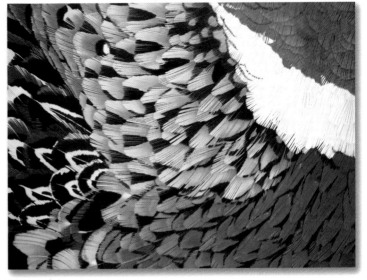

Ring-neck

Darner/Birch

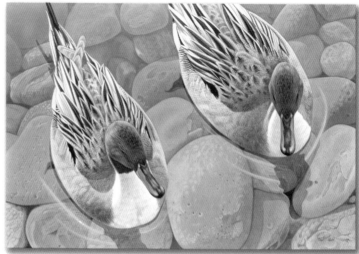

Down on Pintails III

Cecropia/Birch

Wild Turkey/Maple

Ring-neck III

Down on Mallards

Polyphemus/Maple

Overlay-Bluejay

Artist's Statement

Creating is an addiction–with all the highs and lows you would expect. I am interested in the surface textures and creating paintings that portray them in realistic detail. Hopefully a viewer will feel they can run a hand over the feathers and moss, or grasp an object in the painting.

This detail is usually composed in an abstract design. The design can occur naturally or be arranged by me.

The subjects of my paintings are usually based on nature and sometimes manmade objects. I have found subjects to paint in remote wilderness areas of the world, local parking lots and my own backyard. *–Rick Pas*

www.RickPas.com

Quiet Sports
The Dragonfly's Water Dance

The blue cloud hovered over the mud puddle. It burst apart as my mountain bike bounced, then splashed, through the water. Dozens of butterflies flitted around me. Their delicate wings sliced through the air, so close I imagined a soft caress. I pedaled past them and they rejoined, becoming a cloud once again and settling near the water.

I hesitated, straddling my bike, and turned around. A butterfly fluttered its wings and rose, but the others were still. They appeared as one being, a giant winged creature of a blue so extraordinary it seemed not of this Eearth.

The moment felt like a gift, as if I had tumbled into a favorite storybook: *The Secret Garden* mixed with a dash of *The Wizard of Oz.* The charm of quiet sports unfolded around me. By treading softly, I had been rewarded with a peek into a magical world.

Few creatures whisper magic like the butterfly and its winged friends. I had never thought much about these insects until we bought our house in northern Michigan. There, among the red pines and restless wind, they gather like welcome guests, friends returning after the brutality of winter.

A few years ago, while paddling the headwaters of northeastern Michigan's Ocqueoc River, I rounded a corner and encountered dozens of green dragonflies. My paddle dangled in my fingers, and they descended upon my kayak. I drifted in the narrow river. Their wings vibrated in the sun, and they moved constantly, sensing what I was unable to see.

Last summer zebra-striped dragonflies zipped along while I paddled the Upper Peninsula's Indian River. At times they crashed into me, their bodies feeling strangely powerful. And on northeastern Michigan's Black River, butterflies flounced among white pom-pom flowers, the scene so perfect it belonged in a children's picture book.

These winged creatures are nature's showstoppers, never failing to entertain. Returning one evening from a hike, my headlamp caught a giant, brown moth gathered on our porch. Attracted to the light splashing from inside, it looked almost prehistoric. Petite pink and yellow moths rested nearby.

On another kayak trip, my paddle skimmed over northern Michigan's Lake Emma. Drops flew in the air, and I noticed a black and white dragonfly playing in the spray. It flitted here and there, in and out of the moisture. I paused, captivated by the charm of a dragonfly's water dance, another opportunity to see how magical, how astonishing the world really is.

–Erin Fanning

As a child, it was a summer ritual I shared with other neighborhood kids: secking butterflies on the wing. Seeing them was a thrill, though in my still-forming mind they were also nothing more than a beautiful curiosity. They were beauty taken for granted—and sometimes captured for a naïve thrill. Their beauty was always fascinating, with the erratic zig-zags of color they painted transiently upon the air.

In the ensuing years I've learned to look more deeply into the world, and when I look at the living art of butterflies now, I see beauty that extends beyond simple forms of color. It's easy to see the beauty of lightness: that aerial dance we can only dream of doing. I also see the beauty of small strength: In the ability of some butterflies to migrate vast distances, I take inspiration for our own abilities to travel beyond imagination. Life's beautiful interconnection is on clear display as well, as butterflies do their part by nurturing the plants, and by sacrificing their lives to creatures who eat them–and to little boys who capture them. The artful beauty of life itself is on perfect display in the miraculous intricacies of their tiny wings and bodies.

The world's best art tends to have layers of meaning and message, able to be appreciated for its sheer beauty, yet also communicates on other levels to those who care to explore its depth. The masterpieces of butterflies are no exception: With their delicacy and endangerment, they paint a picture of the fragility of individuals and the entire living system. As an indicator species that is in decline in many areas, they speak of the perils of our own journeys as well as their own. Without a preaching word, they give us with their beauty an opportunity for awareness of all that we, in our continued naïveté, may inadvertently capture.

Yes, for the all the skills of consciousness we've developed, often we're still just larger little boys–and girls–with beauty in a jar, unsure of all we've captured; our admiration of beauty doesn't impede our accidental killing of it. And when I look to the skies that the free butterflies still inhabit, I see we're in the jar ourselves—the jar of Earth's tiny atmosphere, where our own fragile beauty needs as much respectful care as theirs. It's times like those when I most need the summer miracle of a swallowtail flitting by, out of reach of any but the breeze.

–Eric Alan is author/photographer of the book Wild Grace: Nature as a Spiritual Path (White Cloud Press). *eric@wildgrace. com or www.wildgrace.org*

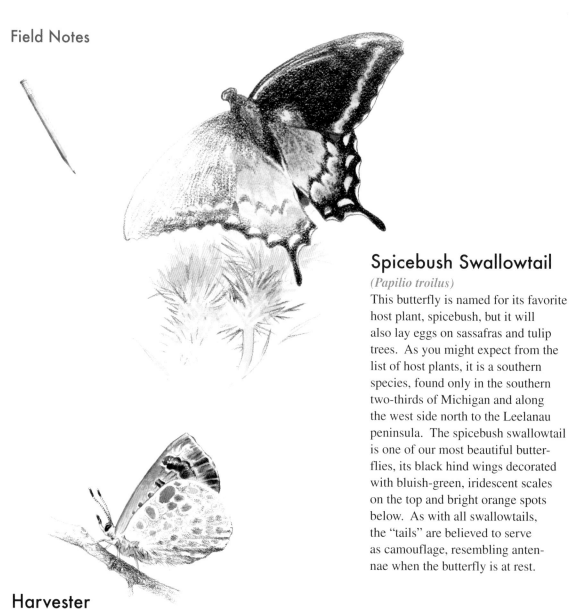

Spicebush Swallowtail
(Papilio troilus)

This butterfly is named for its favorite host plant, spicebush, but it will also lay eggs on sassafras and tulip trees. As you might expect from the list of host plants, it is a southern species, found only in the southern two-thirds of Michigan and along the west side north to the Leelanau peninsula. The spicebush swallowtail is one of our most beautiful butterflies, its black hind wings decorated with bluish-green, iridescent scales on the top and bright orange spots below. As with all swallowtails, the "tails" are believed to serve as camouflage, resembling antennae when the butterfly is at rest.

Harvester
(Feniseca tarquinius)

"Meat eater" is not a phrase generally used to describe a butterfly, but in the case of the harvester, it is accurate at least for the larval stage. Larvae feast exclusively on woolly alder aphids. You have to look closely to spot a harvester caterpillar, as its white color blends well with the white, cottony appearance of the aphids. It is not a tidy eater, getting quite messy from the sugary secretions of the aphids as it plows its way through the herd. The adult harvester is also dependent on aphids for food, but with a proboscis rather than chewing mouth parts, it contents itself with the aphids' honeydew secretions.

Monarch

(Danaus plexippus)

The big eyes that seem to make up the entire head of butterflies can lead us to believe their world is a mostly visual one. But in fact, they are just as tuned into the chemical world. Monarchs, for instance, have chemoreceptors on their antennae and on all six legs. Females use receptors on their legs to determine whether a plant has the right chemical makeup to lay eggs on. For instance, a female can determine whether a plant is milkweed and whether it is healthy. The receptors on her antennae detect the presence of a male Monarch, who releases a pheromone from scent glands on his hind wings.

Eastern Pine Elfin

(Incisalia niphon)

As its name implies, the eastern pine elfin is dependent on pine trees. New growth on small trees is the preferred target, with the tiny first instars boring into the needles to feed. Later instars are large enough to eat the needle from the tip down. Caterpillars are bright green with noticeable cream-colored stripes running the length of the body. This is one of Michigan's earliest butterflies of the spring; adults take flight in mid-April, and they are seldom found past June.

Viceroy

(Limenitis archippus)

If you go looking for a viceroy caterpillar or chrysalis, set your specific search image to "bird dropping," as both are well-camouflaged to look like a fresh deposit from their avian predators. Viceroys overwinter as early instar caterpillars, creating a shelter, which is called a hibernaculum, by rolling a small leaf and attaching it to the stem of a small willow, aspen or poplar with silk. After further developing in the spring, the caterpillar forms a brown and white chrysalis, which hangs from a twig or a blade of grass. The chrysalis looks very much like a tiny bird dropping with a pair of black, branched spines coming out over the head.

Great Spangled Fritillary

(Speyeria cybele)

The highly visible adult of this species is a harsh contrast to its seldom-seen caterpillar, which feeds at night and hides in piles of rocks, brush or logs during the day. You are very likely hosting these caterpillars if you have even a small patch of violets in your yard or woods. Females lay up to 2,000 eggs in the fall, in the vicinity of, but not directly on, a patch of violets. The eggs hatch soon afterward, and the larvae hibernate for the winter. Look for them at night amongst your violets--black caterpillars with orange heads and rows of black and orange spines.

Painted Lady

(Vanessa cardui)

The painted lady is one of our most common butterflies, yet lepidopterists are having an increasingly difficult time studying its migratory behavior. It is a lover of open areas, nectaring on thistle, milkweed, joe-pye weed, aster and other sun-loving flowers. The difficulty arises from the proliferation of butterfly dealers, who sell this and other butterflies by the tens of thousands for release at weddings and other outdoor events. This seems like a harmless business practice, but such releases make it impossible to accurately track the movements of this migrant species. It is likely resulting in a mix of genes and migration patterns from different populations.

Hummingbird Clearwing

(Hemaris thysbe)

The hummingbird clearwing moth is one of the few members of the hawk moth family that flies during the day. It wasn't surprising, therefore, for researchers to learn that these moths see a broad spectrum of color, including yellow, blue and green. But the next discovery was a surprise to all–it turns out that the moths in the study can also see colors at night, enough to distinguish blue objects from a series of gray backgrounds, even in near total darkness! The mechanism is still a mystery, but researchers believe moths store visual signals until the signal is strong enough to register a color.

by Janea Little of the Chippewa Nature Center, Midland, Michigan
Artwork by Rod Lawrence

Survival Skills
Firemaking: An Ancient Story

Long ago, our ancient ancestors passed on stories about fire making. Each story was a blueprint used by the practitioner to remember all the crucial steps involved to achieve success. They also, through experimentation, knew how this story could be applied to the host of natural materials that were found in their area. Whether the story was literal or metaphorical, it conveyed instructions on how this gift could be brought to the people.

Here is the story I learned. The spindle, which is the male part, is spun on top of the fireboard, the female part, and heat is generated. With each pass of the spindle, the heat increases, tearing small particles from the fireboard. The notch focuses the heat by collecting the hot particles; this is called birthing a coal. The coal is transferred to the tinder bundle where air, the breath of life, is blown into the tinder. The tinder fibers are heated up and transformed into a gas. As the rising column of gas thickens and heats up, fire is created.

To create fire, four things need to be present for combustion to happen. They are:
1. A hot spot
2. Air
3. Fuel
4. An uninhibited chain reaction

These four aspects are called the tetrahedron of fire making and are interdependent. No one is greater than the other, but if one is missing, the fire making process will not happen. Fire by friction is more than rubbing two sticks together and hoping for the best. It is a complex series of events. If you want to create fire like the ancient ones, research what techniques and materials the indigenous people of the Great Lakes used, and still use today in some ceremonies. Making fire using ancient skills is an experience that awakens a long forgotten story within each of us.
–*Shawn Grose*

As summer's warmth beckons us to be outdoors, it's important to remember that amidst the burst of flora and fauna are easily unseen insects with the potential to transmit disease. Ticks are second only to mosquitoes as vectors of human disease. They are often found in tall grass, where they will rest themselves at the tip of a blade so as to attach themselves to a passing animal or person. A harpoon-like structure in their mouth allows firm anchoring for them to bloat their bodies on a meal of blood. Duration of attachment and release of saliva increase the chance of transmitting organisms that cause deadly diseases. These preventive measures reduce your risk of infection from ticks:

- Wear light-colored clothing with a tight weave (to spot ticks more easily and prevent contact with the skin).
- Wear enclosed shoes.
- Wear long pants tucked into socks, and long-sleeved shirts tucked into pants.
- Use a tick repellent (according to manufacturer's instructions).
- Stay on cleared, well-worn trails whenever possible, and avoid sitting directly on the ground.
- Conduct a full-body check after being in areas likely to have ticks (tall grass, leaf litter and shrubs). Be sure to check the scalp, neck, in the ears, behind joints, and in the groin.

If you find an embedded tick, sometimes no larger than a sesame seed, remove it promptly:

- Use fine-tipped tweezers to grasp the tick as close to the skin as possible and pull upward with steady, even pressure (do not twist or jerk the tick).
- Do not squeeze, crush, or puncture the tick's body (to prevent release of infectious body contents).
- After removing the tick, thoroughly disinfect the bite site and wash your hands with soap and water.
- Place the tick in a container and put it in your freezer. Include information about the date and body location of the bite (to give to your physician if signs or symptoms of tick-borne illness occur).

Note: Folklore remedies such as petroleum jelly or nail polish may increase the risk of infection by irritating the tick, which stimulates release of additional saliva.

Notify your physician if a tick bite is followed by rash, fever, chills, headache, muscle aches, joint pain and inflammation, vomiting, fatigue, or swollen lymph nodes.

–Nancy Bordine, R.N.

Curious Wonders
Was it Something They Ate?

The bright blue tropical butterfly *Morpho* has stimulated creative study by naturalists and scientists for centuries. However, one does not have to travel to the tropics to enjoy the enchantment of a flying bit of iridescent blue. A velvet-winged, black-as-coal butterfly with neon highlights can lead you just as well through the open woodlands of temperate North America. It is the the red-spotted purple.

As I enjoyed the colors glinting off some of these hiking companions on one bright summer day, I became curious. When a group of them settled to probe a hairy old rope of coyote scat, I noticed that while most flashed a pure silvery blue, others showed fluorescent blue-green, golden-green, or greenish-orange. Did the different colors come from structural arrangements on the scales or was it something they ate?

I soon learned that the atomic structure of melanin pigments creates black, brown and gray. White, cream and yellow comes from flavonoid pigments. The greater the flavonoid content in a scale, the yellower the wings. Butterflies probably get their flavonoids from the plants they eat. By developing warning color patterns, these pigments can make a predator hesitate. Their bright flash of color might also help them find a mate. And pigments may protect their cells from ultraviolet damage. Scientists are studying whether flavonoid pigments also protect butterflies from microbial attacks. Using what they learn from butterflies, chemists then hope to figure out how to protect us from ultraviolet light as well as from some forms of disease.

Although bioterin is found in the blue of *Morpho* wings, the blue color reflected off our northern charmer may come from some other collection of atoms. Various bile pigments have been isolated from blue scales. Science suggests that the minerals and salt ions that these butterflies need to produce blue aren't concentrated enough in the nectars of flowering willows, poplars, cherries and other food trees. Therefore, my companions probably were probing the coyote scat for the missing atoms.

The colors we see reflected from a butterfly wing are actually formed by a combination of pigments and prism-like reflections. Red-spotted purple butterflies may gather their black, gray, orange and white colors from a variety of sources. As they gathered on the coyote scat, however, I think they were seeking a bit of blue to make their scales shine.
–*Jody M. Clark*

Recently my children and I had fun playing with butterflies in the indoor Michigan 4H Children's Garden on the Michigan State University campus. During the winter months, when the outdoor garden is barren, you can still enjoy the 4H Children's Garden. The staff has turned one of the greenhouse rooms of the Plant & Soil Sciences Building into a lovely garden complete with potting shed, pond, paths, mini-greenhouse and lots of tropical and blooming plants. During March and April they also turn it into delightful butterfly habitat for their Butterflies in the Garden program.

The experience made me excited for spring to arrive, but it also served to remind me of all the elements necessary to make butterflies at home in your garden. They are: water, food, shelter and caterpillar host plants.

My son, Peter, was fascinated by watching the butterflies alight on a plastic pot scrubber sitting in a pool of water in a little plastic dish. These were scattered throughout the garden for puddling, or creating a perch from which the butterflies could take a sip of water.

A large sign explained what butterflies liked to eat, in other words nectar plants: petunia, bee balm, cosmos, black-eyed susans, salvia, borage, agastache and heliotrope to name a few. Many were in evidence as the children excitedly followed the butterflies throughout the space. I have also seen butterflies enjoy Nicotiana and impatiens in my garden.

Lush plantings can provide shelter for butterflies from the sun or predators, but you can also include a butterfly box. This resembles a long thin birdhouse with long slats cut into it instead of round holes. The Children's Garden had a cheery painted butterfly house mounted one about one foot off the ground in a flower bed.

And of course, if you want butterflies to take up residence in your garden and not merely pass through, you must provide a host plant for their young. Many herbs, such as parsley and fennel, are desirable host plants.

Probably the most important thing to do to make butterflies welcome is to be an organic gardener. Pesticides and herbicides are harmful to our gossamer garden friends. 🦋
–*Michelle Worden, MSUE*
Master Gardener Volunteer

Backyard Birds
Baltimore Oriole–A Brilliant Bird

The baltimore oriole takes the orange and black coloration of monarch and baltimore butterflies to the extreme: On adult males, the black is dark and velvety while the orange is nearly fluorescent. They don't achieve these colors until after their second summer, but it's well worth the wait. Even a few females get this bright, but it takes much longer. Both bird and butterfly were named for Maryland's colonial proprietor, Lord Baltimore, whose colors were orange and black.

Much like their butterfly namesake, the baltimore oriole drinks nectar, even smashing flowers to extract the juice. Fruits are also preferred, especially dark-colored ones, and the oriole will eat them whole or by gaping, which is piercing the rind and opening its beak to lap up the resulting mashed pulp and juice. During the summer, though, the main foods are caterpillars, spiders and insects. Young birds grow incredibly fast, and they need all the protein the adults can deliver. In springs with caterpillar outbreaks, local oriole populations increase.

The pendant nest is an engineering marvel, often lasting a year or more. The female is the sole builder, sometimes traveling one-quarter mile to find just the right materials. The nest is often built in the same tree as last year's nest, and the female will simply reuse hard-to-find materials. The outer layer contains long, strong grasses tangled and woven together to be slightly stretchy. Strands from horses' manes and tails are highly prized. The inside layer is shorter, finer grass, while the lining is soft fluffy down from cattails or cottonwoods. Even while she's incubating her eggs, the female will be busy weaving loose ends back into the nest wall.

Of the six orioles native to North America, the baltimore is the most striking. The large scattered trees of established suburban neighborhoods are fine habitat for them, so they can be spotted just about anywhere. However, this jewel-bright bird isn't often seen, as it spends most of its time in the high treetops, and it rarely sings after nesting starts in earnest. Even the nest is often concealed. Be prepared for a surprise: If you look, you may find you have the prettiest bird in town for a neighbor.
–*Torrey Wenger*

Torrey Wenger writes from the Kalamazoo Nature Center in Kalamazoo, Michigan.

Baltimore Oriole

(Icterus galbula)

Length: 8.75 inches
Wing span: 11.5 inches
Weight: 1.2 ounces

Adult male: Head hooded in black, wings black with orange shoulders and white bars, lower back and underparts orange, tail orange with black center.
Adult female: Same color scheme as adult male but more pale. Black replaced by mottled brown, and orange is faded. No orange shoulder patches on wings.
Juvenile: Similar to adult female but even more pale. Juvenile females have most pale color. Males take two years to acquire adult plumage.

Voice: Short whistled phrases in a rich, clear voice. Each male has unique songs, although neighbors may share a repertoire. Females can also sing but usually give shorter calls.
Behavior: Arrives in May and leaves in August. Spends most of its time in the treetops but occasionally forages on the ground. Generally solitary, although fledglings gather in small flocks before they migrate.
Mating/Breeding: Monogamous. Males arrive first and vigorously court females as they arrive. Males sing and bow; receptive females chatter in response. All females in an area lay eggs at about the same time. Both adults join multi-species flocks to mob predators near the nest.

Nest: The female weaves a hanging, purse-like nest lined with plant down.
Fledge: 11 to 14 days. Young noisy right before and after fledging.
Food: Nectar, fruit, caterpillars, spiders and insects.
Habitat: Edges of woods and open woods, especially near water.
Breeding range: Most of the eastern U.S. and central Canada.

Musings of Dewitt Jones, Photographer
Hope

My back hurts! I wish I could say I just strained it during a good hard hike, or carrying my cameras to the top of some fabulous mountain, but it's deeper than that. I've had an unfused lumbar vertebra since birth (spondylolisthesis) and, as I get older, it's finally catching up to me.

I've tried everything except surgery and it still hurts. The odds are good that the pain will just be part of my life going forward.

So how does one deal? I'm a pretty optimistic guy, but there are days when it really gets me down, makes me feel about 100 years old, darkens every step I take. Optimism? Come on, how many affirmations can you intone before your brain starts screaming, "Hey, it HURTS! Don't tell me it's all getting better, that it will all be just fine! It hurts! Make it stop!"

It's at times like these that I'm really glad I'm a nature photographer. Not so much the photographer part, but the nature part. I've spent my life hanging out among trees and waves and mountains, and it's the lessons I've learned there that really help me now.

I recently read a quote by Vaclav Havel that articulated a feeling that I've so often had while wandering in nature. "Hope," he said, "is definitely not the same thing as optimism. Hope is not the conviction that something will turn out well, but the certainty that something makes sense, regardless of how it turns out."

I sit in nature surrounded by flowers and songbirds, clouds and granite, bracken and bacteria. Held in that great panoply of wonder and possibility, the smile that graces my face *is* one of hope–a certainty that it all makes sense from the macro to the micro; from the heavens to my unfused disk.

I know others looking at the same scene have found quite the opposite. Nature is a scary place for them. The law of the jungle: eat or be eaten. Hope? Forget it. Life is nothing more than the chaos of atoms bumping into each other. No sense here, just nonsense.

Even Barak Obama called his new book, *The Audacity of Hope*. Great book, but "audacity"? Not for me. Too much time hanging out in wilderness, too much time drinking in the beauty. The way I read it, nature publishes hope everyday.

I remember one night while teaching a seminar at Point Reyes National Seashore stepping out into the parking lot behind the visitor's center to take a break from my students. It had been a long day–technical problems with my projector, one lady had turned her ankle on a hike. Just life,

but enough chaos to make me start to doubt myself and what I was doing. Had I lost hope? No, but I didn't quite "have" hope either. I headed over to my car to get a folder of notes. Then, as I turned back, there before me the new moon was setting over the ridgeline. I grabbed my camera.

From my right, a single cloud appeared–the only one in the entire sky. Wistfully, almost playfully, it skipped–O.K. maybe a cloud can't skip, but this one did! It skipped along the tops of the trees. When it reached the perfect point between trees and moon, it actually seemed to hesitate. "Come on, push the shutter!" it called. I did. Then, not with a voice but with a feeling deep in my heart, it seemed to add "It all makes sense, on levels you can't even imagine. If you forget, just come back outside and I'll remind you."

I walked back to my class with hope in my heart and a heck of a shot in my camera.

Optimism and pessimism are mental attitudes. Hope may have a mental component as well, but it seems larger than that. A bowl large enough to hold both optimism and pessimism, both yin and yang–hold them in the soul's deep resonance with the underlying nature of things.

We often lose our optimism when we feel we've lost control of our lives. But in the final analysis, perhaps it was folly to think we ever could "control" them. There are far too many unintended con-sequences and unfused vertebrae.

However, we *can* control our perspective–and the perspective I find in nature joyously confirms my sense of hope, over and over and over again.
–Dewitt Jones

You can learn more about Dewitt Jones at www.DewittJones.com

Folklore

Butterflies as Souls: An Ancient Legend of Metamorphosis

A creature as lovely as the butterfly is bound to be linked with beautiful stories. One of the most celebrated comes to us from the ancient Mediterranean, where the word psyche meant soul. The soul was often shown as a butterfly flying away from the body; likewise, the goddess Psyche has sometimes been shown in art, both ancient and more recent, with butterfly wings.

The story of the goddess Psyche was told about two thousand years ago by the Roman Apuleius in his book *Metamorphoses.* Although most of the book has a satirical edge, this story has a deep and serious meaning to it.

Many elements in the story are interchangeable with our well-known fairy tales. Psyche starts out as the youngest daughter of a king, and she is so beautiful that the love goddess Venus is full of envy. Venus's son, Cupid, is supposed to punish Psyche for this, but he falls in love with her instead. What happens next includes plotting stepsisters and Venus's acting like a wicked stepmother.

Psyche can't join Cupid as his true wife unless she becomes a goddess. To do this she takes on difficult tasks, including a journey to the Land of the Dead. After these nearly impossible missions, Psyche's persistence and love for Cupid pays off. She is granted her godesshood.

Her story symbolizes both the butterfly and the soul in how she must better herself. Like a butterfly, she sheds her former skin. As butterflies were once mere caterpillars, Psyche was once a mere human. She rises above in the skies like a butterfly who has just gotten its wings. The soul was associated with both Psyche and butterflies, not only because it would pass on someday, but because people aimed to better their souls and make them more beautiful.

In the end, Psyche's life turns out lovely. Jupiter, the king of the gods, allows her to join her beloved Cupid, and Venus overcomes her envy and welcomes her new daughter-in-law. Although a butterfly's life is short, Psyche's life now lasts forever. The story of her life will continue forever as well, with people reading it now just as they did in Roman times. The gorgeousness of the butterfly, and its fascinating way of living, makes way for art, stories, and of course, legends. Naturally a legend of Psyche–and the butterfly–would belong in a book called *Metamorphoses*, as we see the metamorphoses in our natural world.

–*Danica Davidson*

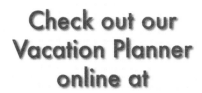

Travel Planner

Complete Your Collection Today!

Life in a Pond
Volume 5 No. 2

Gazing beneath the surface we discover our muse, intimations of our ancestors, the roots of our legends, and reflections of ourselves–and that the surface is but an illusion

Wolves of Isle Royale
Volume 5 No. 3

As messengers of the spirit world, wolves echo our untamed inner instincts, conjure the moon and offer equanimity with their dignity, grace and beauty

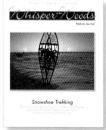

Snowshoe Trekking
Volume 5 No. 4

The solitude of snowshoes atop a sparkling quilt of shadows spilled in soothing hues deepens our perception, transforming the familiar to the new

The Healing Power of Nature
Volume 6 No. 1

Water's sparkling trickle soothes our troubles, fresh air restores our every particle, soft earth absorbs our cares, forests offer patient wisdom–Nature's caress is our ultimate healer

Buying Tip: Caring for Live Mealworms

All sizes of mealworms can be stored for several weeks in refrigeration. If you get them pre-packaged in a plastic cup, just simply put them in the refrigerator. If you buy them bulk and they come in a mesh bag, first remove the bag from the box and let them sit at room temperature. Then place them in the refrigerator for a few hours. Transfer them to a shallow, smooth-sided tray or tub. If the sides of your container are smooth enough, a lid should not be necessary. If a lid is used, it should be well-ventilated or your mealworms will become damp and die in a short time. Add a little bran, oatmeal or cornmeal. Remove your meal-worms from the refrigerator once every 7 to 10 days, let them warm up to room temperature, then feed them a carrot for a few hours. This is how they get their drink of water, and will stay fresh and plump. For more information, call Nature's Way at (800) 318-2611.

The Gift of Nature

Life in a Pond

As a gift for your family or friends, or even as a gift to yourself, *Whisper in the Woods* is a promise of quiet sunrises and gentle breezes.

Subscribers will enjoy the added benefit of receiving a collector's art print yearly.

Call Toll-Free
to Subscribe

(866) 943-0153

Subscribe online
www.WhisperintheWoods.com